LOST CITIES

BY SUE HAMILTON

Published by ABDO Publishing Company, 8000 West 78th Street, Suite 310, Edina, Minnesota 55439.
Copyright ©2008 by Abdo Consulting Group, Inc. International copyrights reserved in all countries.
No part of this book may be reproduced in any form without written permission from the publisher.
Abdo & Daughters™ is a trademark and logo of ABDO Publishing Company.

Printed in the United States.

Editor: John Hamilton
Graphic Design: Sue Hamilton
Cover Design: Neil Klinepier
Cover Illustration: Machu Picchu, Corbis
Interior Photos and Illustrations: p 4 Satellite view of Machu Picchu, ©2006 GeoEye; p 5 (inset photo) Machu Picchu 1911, courtesy Machu Picchu Tourist and Travel Information, Machu Picchu, Peru; Machu Picchu, Corbis; p 6 Poseidon statue, ©2007 Andrew Hilton; Atlantis Hotel aquarium, Corbis; p 8 Excavation of Akrotiri on Santorini, ©2007 William Wallace; p 9 Minoan *Toreador Fresco*, Corbis; p 10 Pyramid of the Masks, ©2007 Philip Baird; p 11 Mayan mask sculpture, ©2007 Philip Baird; p 12 King Arthur tapestry, Corbis; p 13 Corfe Castle, iStockphoto; p 14 Queen Elizabeth I, North Wind Picture Archives; p 15 Walter Raleigh, North Wind Picture Archives; p 16 Scene from *The Road to El Dorado*, courtesy Dreamworks SKG; p 17 Walter Raleigh and his expedition in South America, North Wind Picture Archives; p 18 *Lost Horizon* book cover, courtesy HarperCollins Publishers; Hunza Valley, Corbis; p 19 James Hilton, Corbis; p 20 Charles Boyer, Corbis; p 21 China near the Tibetan border, AP Images; p 22 Camel Tracks near Ubar, NASA; Saudi Arabia map, Cartesia/Hamilton; p 23 Camel train, iStockphoto; p 24 Radar image of area surrounding Ubar, JPL NASA; p 25 Enhanced optical image of area surrounding Ubar, JPL NASA; Ubar excavation, NASA; p 26 Map of Yonaguni, Cartesia/Hamilton; pp 26-29 All underwater Yonaguni photos, ©2007 Shun Daichi.

Library of Congress Cataloging-in-Publication Data

Hamilton, Sue L., 1959-
   Lost cities / Sue Hamilton.
       p. cm. -- (Unsolved mysteries)
   Includes index.
   ISBN 978-1-59928-832-1
   1. Geographical myths--Juvenile literature. 2. Lost continents--Juvenile literature. I. Title.

GR940.H367 2008
398.23'4--dc22
                                        2007014556

CONTENTS

LOST CITIES

How do you lose a city? With today's technology—tracking devices, heat-sensitive locators, global positioning systems—it seems impossible to lose something so big. But hundreds of years ago, cities did indeed disappear. Some were mysteriously abandoned. Many cities were destroyed because of violent wars. Others were deserted because of famine or disease.

Whatever the reason, complete cities disappeared, abandoned by all who once lived there. Some were lost to the swirling yellow sands of the desert, others vanished into the cold blue depths of the oceans, and still others disappeared behind green walls of thick-growing jungle plants. Stories and rumors are all that remain of these once-thriving places.

Lost cities attract both the curious and the greedy. Some stories lead people to believe that great wealth is to be found in these abandoned places. As early as the 16th century, Spanish conquistadors began searching for El Dorado, a South American city reportedly made of gold.

Below: A satellite image by GeoEye of Machu Picchu, Peru.

Machu Picchu

Some lost cities have been rediscovered. Machu Picchu, the lost city of the Incas, was found in 1911. Perched high on a mountain ridge in Peru, its buildings and streets are now filled with archaeologists, researchers, and historians, all trying to find out exactly what happened to this city and its people.

Other places remain out of reach. Even today, researchers and treasure hunters seek the legendary underwater city of Atlantis. From the Mediterranean Sea to the Caribbean Sea, they continue searching for this sunken city. But did Atlantis ever really exist? Is El Dorado out there—a city of gold waiting to be found? Or is it only a legend? There are many questions, some guesses, and a few answers in the unsolved mysteries of these and other lost cities.

Above Inset: Machu Picchu, the lost city of the Incas, when it was found in 1911.
Above: Machu Picchu today. Its secrets are still being uncovered nearly a century later.

ATLANTIS: THE CITY UNDER THE SEA

The island city of Atlantis has fascinated, bewildered, and inspired people for thousands of years. The tale of this lost city was probably first told by ancient Egyptians. Later, the story was written down by Plato, a great teacher who lived in Greece from 427 B.C. to about 347 B.C. Plato wrote that Poseidon, the Greek god of the sea, created Atlantis. The island featured protecting circles of land and sea, with a palace in the middle. Its citizens were peaceful, smart, artistic, and athletic. But over time the Atlanteans became prideful and self-important. They began to wage war with their neighbors. The gods grew displeased with the Atlanteans. Volcanic eruptions and violent earthquakes shook the land, sending Atlantis and its people to the depths of the sea.

Some researchers say that Atlantis never really existed. They believe that Plato simply wrote a morality tale, a fiction story that shows the consequences of how people behave. Other researchers point out that Plato was very specific about the size and location of Atlantis.

Facing Page: The Atlantis Hotel, a resort in the Bahamas, created this aquarium to resemble the fabled lost city. *Below:* A statue of Poseidon. The Greek god of the sea created Atlantis.

Above: Excavation of the village of Akrotiri, on Santorini. Around 1550 B.C. the island, then known as Thera, exploded in one of the biggest volcanic eruptions in history. Some believe that this event was the inspiration for the lost city of Atlantis.

Plato wrote that "…Atlantis was an island larger than Libya and Asia put together." He also stated that the island was "beyond the Pillars of Heracles." People believe that these pillars refer to what is known today as the Rock of Gibraltar and Mount Hacho near Ceuta, Spain. These promontory landmasses are on either side of the Strait of Gibraltar, an area that connects the Mediterranean Sea and the Atlantic Ocean. But not everyone thinks these details refer to the Strait of Gibraltar. In fact, the search for Atlantis has been conducted in many parts of the world, all the way from the Atlantic Ocean to the Caribbean Sea.

Some people think that when Plato wrote about Atlantis, he was really telling the story of the Minoans, an ancient civilization centered on the island of Crete in the Aegean Sea, the largest of the Greek islands. The Minoans were an advanced, peaceful people, whose culture peaked around 1600 B.C. They had beautiful homes and palaces, created amazing artwork, and lived well off the land and the sea, settling comfortably into many islands in the Aegean.

Around 1550 B.C. (the exact date is unknown), the nearby island of Thera, also known as Santorini, exploded in one of the biggest volcanic eruptions in history. The island broke apart, with large portions sinking into the sea. The Minoan civilization was severely damaged by this disaster. Archaeologists believe the event marked the Minoans' eventual decline and downfall.

Could the eruption be the inspiration for the lost city of Atlantis? Some researchers think so, but others do not. They point out that the timing is wrong. Plato said that Atlantis sank into the sea 10,000 years earlier. However, Thera sank into the ocean only about 1,000 years before Plato's time. A few researchers wonder if the original story's dates, which may have come from stories told by ancient Egyptians, could have been translated incorrectly. The discrepancy might be as simple as Plato getting the numbers mixed up. Other researchers insist that the dates are correct, proving that the Minoans were not the inspiration for Atlantis.

Still, there are lingering clues that hint at similarities between the Minoans and the legendary people of Atlantis. In Plato's story, the Atlanteans were said to be a peaceful people living off the sea, just like the Minoans, who developed major fishing and trading ports. In 1967, Greek archaeologist Spyridon Marinatos excavated Minoan ruins on the shattered island of Thera. None of the pottery and artwork he uncovered showed Minoan warriors or battles.

Below: A copy of the Minoan *Toreador Fresco* showing bull leaping.

This reinforced the belief that the Minoans were a peaceful people, unlike neighboring civilizations such as the Greeks. The people of Atlantis were also said to be peaceful. The Minoan artwork depicted the practice of bull leaping. In Plato's story, Atlanteans were also bull leapers.

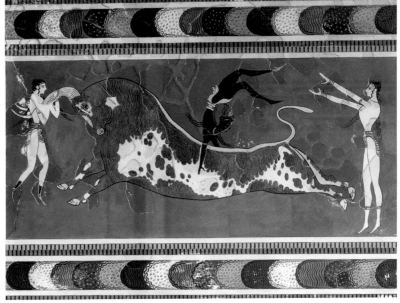

Above: The Pyramid of the Masks at Kohunlich, Mexico. Did the people of Atlantis help the Mayans build this and other pyramids?

Because Plato's stories about Atlantis likely came from ancient Egypt, some people think that Atlanteans influenced Egyptian society in some way. It has even been suggested that it was the Atlanteans who taught the Egyptians how to build pyramids. Halfway around the world, other researchers believe the people of Atlantis also helped the Mayan people build their pyramids. As proof, the researchers point to the Pyramid of the Masks, at Kohunlich, Mexico, in which sculptures are said to depict white gods who came from the sea. However, most archeologists find that both of these theories do not give well-deserved credit to the Egyptian and Mayan people.

Was it really Atlanteans, people displaced from their own land by a devastating volcanic eruption, who arrived to help the natives of these lands create amazing structures? Or did the people of these areas do it on their own? The argument and the search continue while Atlantis remains a lost and unsolved mystery.

Above: A Mayan mask at Kohunlich, Mexico. The sculpture is said to show a white god who came from the sea.

CAMELOT: KING ARTHUR'S CASTLE-CITY

Camelot is the legendary British castle-city of King Arthur and his Knights of the Round Table. Commonly believed to be located somewhere in southern England or Wales, the beautiful castle of Camelot was said to rise above the banks of a nearby river. Plains and dense woods surrounded it. Within its thick walls stood a towering cathedral with bright white towers. Here is where King Arthur and his brave knights gathered, a place of goodness and light amidst the darkness and evil that had spread across the land.

Many historians, however, say Camelot was merely a fictional place, made famous in poems and stories told as far back as the 12th century. The first mention of Camelot was in Chrétien de Troyes' poem *Lancelot, the Knight of the Cart*, written about 1170 A.D. No specifics about Camelot were revealed in the poem, but over the centuries writers and poets have filled in the details.

As for King Arthur, he may have been fictional as well, a warrior-king created in legends and folktales. However, many historians believe that the real-life Arthur may have been a skilled cavalry commander named Artorius. A Briton of Celt ancestry, Artorius was first mentioned in a Welsh poem written by Gododdin around 600 A.D., many years after the great warrior's death. Artorius was a military genius who led his native Britons to victories against invading armies. Fierce and unbeatable, Artorius and his knights brought peace to the land for many years.

Below: King Arthur, a detail from a 14th-century Flemish tapestry. Historians question whether Arthur was a real man or a fictional character.

Was Camelot a place of history or fiction? Some say the village of Caerleon in Wales was the original location of Camelot. However, there are many other places that claim the honor, including Celliwig in Cornwall, Winchester in Wessex, Cadbury Castle in Somerset, and Colchester in east England. Time has blurred the true answer, but archeologists and historians continue searching for King Arthur's lost city of Camelot.

Above: The ruins of Corfe Castle in Dorset, England. Some believe this could have been Camelot.

EL DORADO: THE CITY OF GOLD

Below: Queen Elizabeth I hoped Sir Walter Raleigh would find the lost city of El Dorado and bring back fabulous gold and riches to England.

For hundreds of years, explorers have sought the fabled city of El Dorado. Spanish for "the gilded one," the city was believed to be a place of amazing wealth. In fact, rumors said it was filled with buildings, objects, and streets made of gold. But did El Dorado ever exist? Or was it an exaggeration of an actual place or event?

The legend may have begun with the Spanish conquest of the native Aztec civilization in central Mexico in 1521. It was here that the invaders discovered the remarkable silver and gold

wealth of the New World. The Spaniards heard rumors that more riches existed in the lands to the south. Supposedly, a native king awoke each day, covered himself in gold dust, and each night washed it off, beginning the ritual again the next morning. The rumor set off great explorations in South America.

One of the most famous searchers for El Dorado was Sir Walter Raleigh. An English adventurer, Raleigh had heard tales of the legendary city from Spanish explorers. In 1595, hoping to gain favor with Queen Elizabeth I and acquire some wealth of his own, Raleigh led an expedition to the northern part of South America. After acquiring information from a captured Spanish governor and several native guides, Raleigh's expedition traveled approximately 400 miles (644 km) up the Orinoco River into the country known then as Guiana (modern-day Venezuela).

Above: Sir Walter Raleigh led an expedition to the northern part of South America in 1595 and again in 1616. He hoped to find El Dorado, a city filled with buildings, objects, and streets made of gold.

Above: A scene from Dreamworks' animated motion picture *The Road to El Dorado.*

Raleigh found several tantalizing clues, including traces of gold in the riverbanks and in Indian villages. However, heavy rains and violence by local Indian tribes prevented the group from continuing their search for the fabled city.

Raleigh returned empty-handed to England, intending to go back to South America the following year. However, he was not able to continue the search until 1616. But once again, Raleigh was unsuccessful. The explorer witnessed death and disease in the steamy jungle, but never found El Dorado.

Rumors of the golden city persisted, and many explorers continued seeking the elusive prize. In the early 1600s, a Spanish farmer and shepherd named Juan Rodriguez Freyle owned land near present-day Bogotá, Columbia. In 1636 he wrote a letter to his friend, Don Juan, the governor of Guatavita, a nearby South American city. In the letter, he described an amazing ritual practiced by the Muisca tribe. Freyle wrote that the tribe, when inducting a new leader, "*…anointed him with sticky earth on which they placed gold dust so that he was completely covered with this metal. They placed him on the raft… and at his feet they placed a great heap of gold and emeralds for him to offer to his god. In the raft with him went four principal subject chiefs, decked in plumes, crowns, bracelets, pendants and ear rings all of gold. …When the raft reached the center of the lagoon, they raised a banner as a signal for silence. The gilded Indian then … [threw] out all the pile of gold into the middle of the lake and the chiefs who had accompanied him did the same on their own accounts ….With this ceremony the new ruler was received, and was recognized as lord and king.*"

It did not take long for the governor to pass on this information, and soon Spanish conquistadors raided the Muisca towns. The soldiers took all the gold they could find. They even tried to drain the lake in order to retrieve the treasures they knew rested below the water. The only problem was that the Muisca acquired their gold through trade. They did not have gold mines, nor were their villages filled with buildings or streets of gold. This was not the legendary El Dorado.

The search for the fabulous city of El Dorado continues. Did the city really exist? Is it out there even now, waiting to be found? Some say the wealth of knowledge brought back by the explorers was worth more than the mere metals they sought. But if the city of gold is out there, its location remains an unsolved mystery still today.

Above: Walter Raleigh and his men make plans to find the city of gold and riches in South America.

SHANGRI-LA: WHERE LIFE IS PERFECT

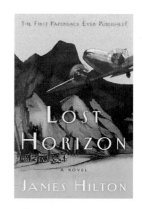

Below: Hunza Valley in northern Pakistan. *Lost Horizon* author James Hilton stayed in the area before he wrote his tale of Shangri-La.

Shangri-La was originally brought to the attention of the world by author James Hilton's 1933 novel *Lost Horizon.* Hilton described Shangri-La as a place lost to the rest of the world. It was a lamasery, a community of Tibetan spiritual leaders called lamas. Hilton wrote that Shangri-La was located in a hidden valley somewhere in the mountains surrounding Tibet. Shangri-La was a utopia—a perfect, peaceful, beautiful place where people aged very slowly, often living for hundreds of years. It was paradise, with plenty of food, libraries filled with books of great knowledge, and enough gold to make each person wealthy.

Above: Lost Horizon told of the hidden city of Shangri-La.

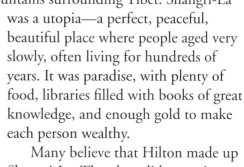

Many believe that Hilton made up Shangri-La. The place did not exist, except in the pages of a book. Others, however, argue that Shangri-La was based on an actual place, a mysterious lost city located somewhere in the Himalayan Mountains.

Some researchers believe the Hunza Valley in northern Pakistan is the basis for Shangri-La. This is due to the fact that James Hilton stayed in the area several years before he wrote his novel.

Above: James Hilton. His 1933 book, *Lost Horizon*, made many people wonder where they could find the beautiful and peaceful place Hilton called Shangri-La.

Although not exactly cut off from the rest of the world, Hunza is surrounded by spectacular mountain peaks, including Rakaposhi, Ultar Sar, Ghenta Peak, Hunza Peak, Darmyani Peak, and Ladyfinger Peak. There are also two ancient forts, the Baltit Fort and the Altit Fort. Surrounded by mountains and not easily accessible, the Hunza Valley seems like a close match to Hilton's description of Shangri-La, but others disagree.

In 1938, German hunter and zoologist Ernst Schäfer traveled to Tibet searching for a lost "master race" of people. Schäfer's expedition was funded by business groups, as well as Heinrich Himmler, the head of the German secret police and the Nazi SS. Schäfer was looking for the homeland of the Aryan race.

Below: Charles Boyer played the High Lama in the 1973 musical movie of *Lost Horizon.*

Many Germans believed the Aryans were a superior group of Caucasian, or "white," people. Schäfer returned to Germany with more than 60,000 photographs and many dozens of reels of film, but no proof that a master race lived hidden from the rest of the world in Shangri-La.

Some say that Shangri-La is simply a place of myth, part of a story. Others insist that it is a real place, perhaps hidden in the heart of India, China, or Tibet. Regardless, Shangri-La continues to be part of an unsolved mystery, a lost city that may be fact or fiction.

Above: Near the Tibetan border in China are beautiful snow-capped mountain peaks, towering Buddhist monasteries, and imposing gorges cut by mighty rivers. Some believe that this is the home of Shangri-La.

UBAR: ATLANTIS OF THE SANDS

Above: Camel tracks leading to Ubar?

For thousands of years the lost city of Ubar, known as the "Atlantis of the Sands," was rumored to be buried somewhere in the Arabian Peninsula. Reportedly, the city developed and grew from about 3000 B.C. to 500 A.D. Then it disappeared, lost in the gritty sands of dust and time. Also called Iram, or Irum, the city of Ubar was thought by some researchers to be a myth. Similar to stories of Atlantis, legend says that God destroyed Ubar because of its people's wrongdoings. Some scientists were convinced it was a real place, once filled with great wealth, and ultimately victim to great tragedy.

Right: Ubar was thought to be in or near the Rub' al Khali (Empty Quarter), a great sea of sand in the southern Arabian Peninsula. This very arid area is roughly the size of Texas, with sand dunes over 600 feet (183 m) high. Searching this vast area was a huge challenge.

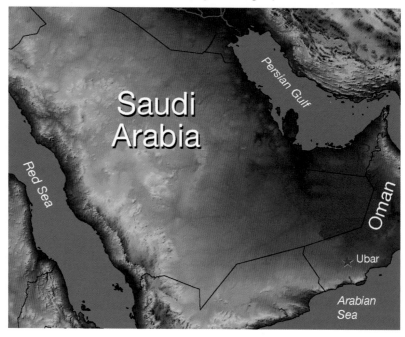

Above: A camel train travels through the desert. Thousands of years ago, caravans traveled to and from Ubar with loads of rare frankincense. Used in incense, perfume, and as a medicine, frankincense trade was a booming business. This brought more people to Ubar. Increased population meant increased water use. This eventually caused the city's destruction.

Located between Africa and Asia, Ubar was a central trading place. Merchants from the Middle East and Europe flocked to the area to conduct business. Great buildings and towers arose, and Ubar became known as the City of a Thousand Pillars. A great eight-sided fort protected caravans traveling with rare frankincense. Ubar was an oasis amidst a desert land. Many researchers wondered what disaster occurred to end the city's rich life. In the 1980s, an answer was finally found.

Right: A radar image taken from the Space Shuttle Endeavour on April 13, 1994, of the region surrounding the lost city of Ubar in Oman in the Arabian Peninsula. The magenta region at the top of the picture shows large sand dunes. The green region is limestone rock on the desert floor. A wadi, or dry riverbed, shown in white, runs through the middle of the image. The actual site of the fortress of Ubar is near the wadi close to the center of the image. Tracks leading to the site appear as reddish streaks.

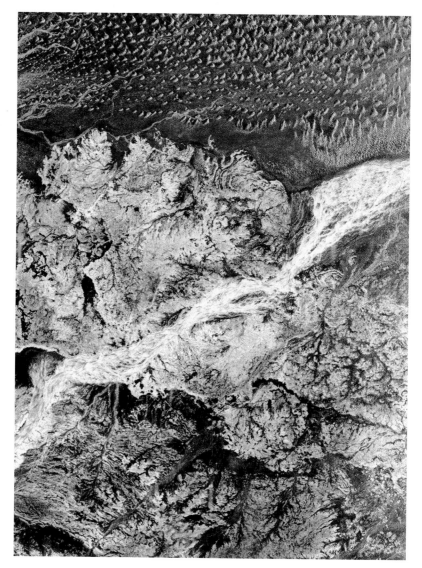

Using ground-penetrating radar to uncover old camel routes, scientists located an old fortress near where the trails came together. This, they believed, was the site of the ancient city of Ubar. After excavating the area, they made an important discovery—a water source. No city could have arisen without fresh water, the most important ingredient for human life. However, the water also turned out to be the source of the city's destruction.

A limestone cavern filled with fresh water was the city's water source. As the city grew, more and more water was consumed. Over the centuries, the water level began to drop. The cavern's roof and walls dried out. It became a giant underground bubble of air.

Left: An enhanced optical image taken by space shuttle astronauts. Although the actual site of the lost city of Ubar is too small to be seen, the white lines are modern roads and old trails that converge into one area.

Below: Since its discovery, archeologists have uncovered many parts of the lost city of Ubar. Below are the remains of a tower, which sat above the vital water hole.

Without the water's support, the cavern finally reached a point where the surrounding ground could no longer support the walls and roof. One day, in a terrifying rumble of rock, dirt, and sand, the cave collapsed, taking the entire city and its people down with it. The water source was buried under tons of rock and wreckage. No water meant no city. The remaining ruins of Ubar were eventually swallowed by sand. A city lost in time.

Ubar remained a lost city for hundreds of years, awaiting modern technology to uncover it once again. But what became of its people? Most likely, those that survived the disaster scattered, taking with them the knowledge of their once-great city.

YONAGUNI: REAL OR MYTH?

Facing Page: A diver explores the neat, terraced steps of what some believe was a building in the lost city of Yonaguni.
Below: A map showing Japan's southernmost island of Yonaguni Jima.

O ff the coast of Japan's southernmost island of Yonaguni Jima, in the blue waters of the East China Sea, there appear to be underwater buildings that may be part of a 10,000-year-old lost city. In 1986, professional scuba diver Kihachiro Aratake was exploring the area, looking for new dive sites, when he passed through an archway. He saw giant stone slabs, perfectly aligned at sharp angles, that seemed very unlike what is typically found in nature. Swimming on, he discovered what seemed to be a drainage ditch that emptied into a small sunken pool. But what amazed him, and the scientists and archeologists who followed, was one huge building with neat, terraced steps. Somewhat similar to the terraced Incan ruins at Machu Picchu, Peru, the pyramid-like monument is about 164 feet (50 m) long and 66 feet (20 m) wide, and climbs 100 feet (30 m) to the water's surface. The site was named Iseki Point. In Japanese, *Iseki* means "historic ruins."

Some scientists guess the buildings may be natural rock formations that were carved into shape long ago by natives of the area. Others argue that the structures are natural rock formations that have been shaped by underwater currents.

Above: Some believe these holes were cut to hold poles for a building.

Some researchers, however, think the stony structures on the sea floor are remains from the lost continent of Mu, an ancient place that sank into the Pacific Ocean, much like the story of Atlantis. For generations, area legends told of an ancient and mysterious "castle under the sea." The place was rumored to have once been home to a group of people who never aged.

Dr. Masaaki Kimura, professor of marine geology at the University of the Ryukyus in Okinawa, began studying the site in 1992. At first, he was not convinced that the Yonaguni Underwater Pyramid was man made. However, his searches have uncovered stone tools and pillars, as well as what appears to be a stone sculpture and a stone tablet carved with symbols that look like a "+" sign, two "O"s, and a ">" sign. In addition, the overall look of the site resembles that of a 14th-century Okinawan castle.

However, geologist Robert Schoch of Boston University is skeptical. He knows that the area's sandstone rocks break cleanly and at sharp angles. He believes that these natural breaks were what created the terraces and stone steps of the Yonaguni Underwater Pyramid.

Another opinion by experienced diver and ancient underwater site specialist Jacques Mayol is that the Yonaguni site is a mixture of natural and man-made formations. In the July 1999 issue of *Diver* magazine, he stated, "I think that the monument at Yonaguni is partly man made. It is absolutely obvious to me that it is not totally natural."

Is this an Atlantis-like lost city? Did a flood or earthquake cause it to end up underwater? The site continues to be studied, but many think that Yonaguni is a lost city waiting to be fully rediscovered.

Left: Turtle Rock in the Yonaguni ruins. Was it cut by people or by nature? Geology experts continue to study the site, looking for an answer.

Above: Large parallel stones are studied by a scuba diver.

GLOSSARY

ARCHAEOLOGIST

A person who searches for, uncovers, and studies artifacts from the past in order to learn how people of ancient societies once lived. Archaeologists try to discover information about an area's people, such as the foods they ate, the kind of homes they lived in, who was in charge, and what was important to them.

ARYAN

A Caucasian, or white-skinned, person who is not of Jewish descent. In the 20th century, Adolf Hitler, leader of Nazi Germany, believed that the Aryans were a race superior to all others.

AZTECS

American Indian people who once controlled much of Mexico and Central America. Their civilization was at its peak until the arrival and conquest of the area by Spanish explorers in the early 16th century.

BULL LEAPING

A sport or religious ritual practiced by the Minoan civilization. The bull leaper would either leap between a bull's horns and land in a handstand on the animal's back or use the bull's horns to catapult himself to a standing position on the bull.

CARIBBEAN

The islands and area of the Caribbean Sea, roughly the area between Florida and South and Central America.

CONQUISTADORS

Spanish soldiers and explorers who came over to Central and South America in the 1500s and used force to conquer native people and take control of their lands.

EXCAVATE

To remove dirt, rock, and other natural materials in a careful and exacting way in order to find buried remains.

FRANKINCENSE

A pleasant-smelling, gum-like substance that comes from Boswellia trees in Africa and Asia. The sticky white resin oozes out of cuts in the trees and hardens as it dries. Frankincense is used in incense and perfume, as well as in medicine for certain illnesses.

GEOLOGIST

A scientist who studies rocks to develop an understanding of the history of Earth.

GILDED

To be thinly covered with gold or gold paint.

Global Positioning System (GPS)

A system of orbiting satellites that transmits information to GPS receivers on Earth. Using information from the satellites, receivers can calculate location, speed, and direction with great accuracy.

Himalayas

A mountain range extending about 1,500 miles (2,414 k) along the border between India and the Tibet region of China, and through Pakistan, Nepal, and Bhutan. The Himalayas contain many of the highest mountain peaks on Earth, including Mount Everest.

Knights of the Round Table

The legendary group of knights who swore loyalty to King Arthur and who lived at the castle-city of Camelot. The Round Table was a large table where many knights could sit together in a circle. In that way, no one knight was more important than another. In addition to King Arthur, some of the most famous knights who sat at the Round Table included Sir Lancelot, Sir Gawain, Sir Gareth, Sir Kay, Sir Bedevere, Sir Bors, and Sir Galahad.

Lamasery

A place where Buddhist spiritual leaders called lamas live together, study, and practice their religion.

Poseidon

In Greek mythology, Poseidon was the god of seas, lakes, and rivers. He is often shown with a trident, or three-pronged spear, in his hand. In Roman mythology, he was called Neptune.

SS

The SS was the German military organization that was part of Germany's Nazi Party. SS stands for *Schutzstaffel*, which means "protective squadron." Members of the SS had a reputation for being intense fighters, but they were also responsible for carrying out some of the most brutal crimes of World War II, including the Holocaust.

Strait of Gibraltar

A narrow channel of water between Africa and Europe. The Strait of Gibraltar is the only waterway that connects the Mediterranean Sea with the Atlantic Ocean.

Tibet

A region in central Asia within China and bordering Nepal and India. The region of Tibet has an average elevation of 16,000 feet (4,877 m), and is called the "Rooftop of the World."

Utopia

An imaginary place where everybody and everything is perfect. The word was first used by author Sir Thomas More in his 1516 book *Utopia*.

Zoologist

A scientist who studies the life and behavior of animals.

INDEX